ABOUT THE AUTHOR

Neil Ardley has written a number of innovative nonfiction books for children, including *The Eyewitness Guide to Music.* He also worked closely with David Macaulay on *The Way Things Work.* In addition to being a well-known author in the fields of science, technology, and music, he is an accomplished musician who composes and performs both jazz and electronic music. He lives in Derbyshire, England, with his wife and daughter.

Project Editor Linda Martin
Editor Jenny Vaughan
Art Editor Peter Bailey
Designer Mark Regardsoe
Photography Dave King
Created by Dorling Kindersley Limited, London

Library of Congress Cataloging-in-Publication Data
Ardley, Neil.
The science book of magnets/Neil Ardley.—1st U.S. ed.
p. cm.
"Gulliver books."
Summary: Simple experiments demonstrate basic principles of magnetism.
ISBN 0-15-200581-1
1. Magnets—Juvenile literature. [1. Magnets—Experiments. 2. Experiments.]
I. Title.
QC757.5.A73 1991
538'.4—dc20   90-48028

Printed in Belgium by Proost
First U.S. edition 1991
A B C D E

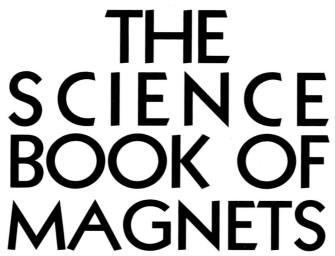

THE SCIENCE BOOK OF MAGNETS

Neil Ardley

HBJ

Gulliver Books

Harcourt Brace Jovanovich, Publishers

San Diego   New York   London

What are magnets?

Magnets have an invisible force that pulls things toward them or pushes things away. This invisible force is used for a variety of purposes. Magnets are used in electric motors that power everything from trains to hair dryers. Magnets in tape and disc players make it possible for us to listen to music. Computers use magnets to record information. The earth itself is a giant magnet, with its own magnetic force.

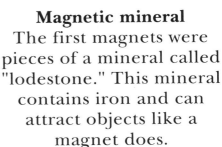

Magnetic mineral
The first magnets were pieces of a mineral called "lodestone." This mineral contains iron and can attract objects like a magnet does.

Lights in the sky
The earth's magnetism causes colored lights to appear in the sky near the north and south poles.

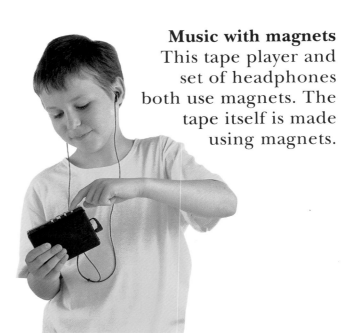

Music with magnets
This tape player and set of headphones both use magnets. The tape itself is made using magnets.

Flying home
Some scientists believe that homing pigeons use the earth's magnetism to help them find their way home.

Magnetic attraction
A magnet easily picks up paper clips. Paper clips are made of steel, and steel is attracted to a magnet.

⚠ This is a warning symbol. It appears within an experiment next to a step that requires caution. When you see this symbol, ask an adult for help.

Be a safe scientist
Follow all the instructions carefully and always use caution, especially with glass, scissors, matches, and electricity.

Take care of magnets. Do not drop them. When you are not using them, put a piece of steel across the ends or stick your magnets together in pairs.

Be careful when you use batteries in experiments—they can make wires very hot.

Sometimes you may need matchsticks to help connect wires to batteries. Make sure you use only <u>used</u> matchsticks.

Funny fish

You can catch fish using a magnet. Start by making your own fishing rod and fish. This will show you how some objects stick to magnets.

You will need:

Bowl of water

Paper

Rod

Tape

Scissors

Horseshoe magnet

Paper clips   Pen or pencil   Thread or string

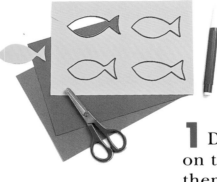

1 Draw some fish on the paper. Cut them out.

2 Slide a paper clip onto each fish.

Put the fish in gently. It does not matter if they sink.

3 Carefully place the fish in the water.

4 Firmly tie one end of the string to the magnet.

5 Tie the other end of the string to the rod. Use tape to keep it from slipping. This is your magnetic fishing rod.

6 Hold the rod over the bowl and lower the magnet. It picks up the fish.

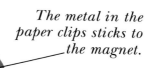

The metal in the paper clips sticks to the magnet.

The magnet works through water, so you can catch any fish that sink.

Magnetic messages
These letters and numbers stick to a refrigerator door. They have magnets inside them. The letters and numbers stick to the door because it is metal.

Magnetic attraction

Do magnets draw everything toward them? Collect some objects made of different materials. Find out which ones a magnet attracts.

You will need:

Horseshoe magnet

Collection of small objects made of different materials

1 Lower the magnet over each object, one at a time.

The ends of the magnet, or "poles," pull the hardest.

A magnet will attract only things made of iron or steel.

A magnet will not attract anything not made of metal.

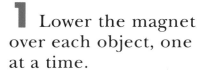

It will not attract all metals.

2 Some of the objects stick to the magnet. Others do not.

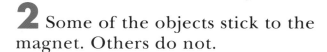

High flier

How far does a magnet's power reach? A magnet can hold something in the air without even touching it. See how a magnet's power, or "magnetism," reaches out and pulls an object toward it.

You will need:

 Paper

 Bar magnet

 Scissors

Tape

Paper clip

 Thread or string

1 Tie the thread to the paper clip. Tape the other end to a table top.

Magnetism passes through air and paper as it pulls the paper clip toward the magnet.

2 Use the magnet to pick up the paper clip. Lift the magnet until the thread is straight.

3 Pull the magnet away from the paper clip. It still holds the paper clip in the air, even when you pass a piece of paper in front of it.

Boat race

A magnet's force can pass through water and some solid materials, as well as through air. You can make a pair of boats that are propelled by the power of magnetism.

You will need

 Two flat sticks or rulers

 Two boat shapes cut from cork or styrofoam

 Two pins

 Tape

Two steel thumbtacks

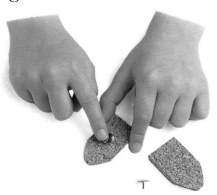 Two large books

Water

Two bar magnets

Scissors

Paper

 Shallow glass or plastic dish

1 Push a thumbtack into each boat.

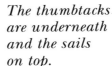
The thumbtacks are underneath and the sails on top.

2 Make paper sails for your boats and attach them with pins.

3 Place the dish across the books and fill it with water.

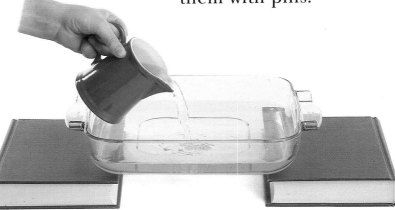

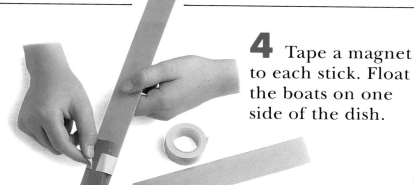

4 Tape a magnet to each stick. Float the boats on one side of the dish.

The magnet's force passes through the bowl and the water to the thumbtacks.

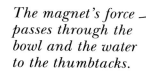

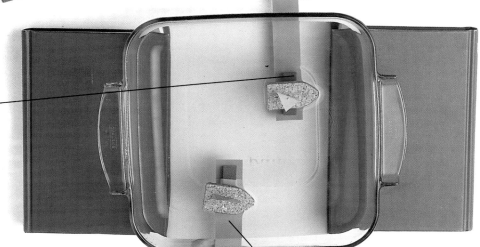

If you move the magnets too quickly, they may get too far away to attract the boats.

5 Race the boats by moving the magnets under the dish. As you move the magnets forward, the boats follow.

Underwater magnets
This diver is testing part of an oil rig, 300 meters (1,000 feet) underwater. The cable used in these tests is held in place by magnets. These work as well underwater as they do on land.

Pair of poles

The two ends, or "poles," of a magnet have different names. One is the north pole and the other is the south pole. Learn how to find out which is which.

You will need:

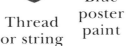

Thread or string

Blue poster paint

Paintbrush

Compass

Bar magnet

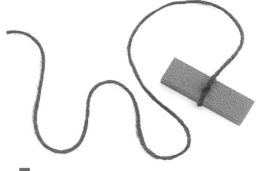

1 Tie the thread around the center of the magnet so that it balances.

Use a compass to find north.

2 Hang the magnet up and let it settle. Be sure there is no metal nearby.

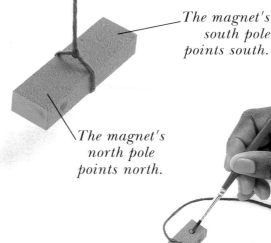

The magnet's south pole points south.

The magnet's north pole points north.

3 Paint the end pointing south blue.

Magnetic compass
A compass needle is a magnet with its north pole at its tip. Therefore, it always points north.

14

Poles apart

Magnets attract other things, but not always each other. They may pull each other together, but they can also push apart, or repel, each other. Whether they attract or repel each other depends on their poles.

You will need:

Two bar magnets with their poles marked (see page 14)

South pole

North pole

Unlike poles (north-south or south-north) always attract each other.

1 Put the magnets on a table, with a north pole facing a south pole. Slide them toward each other. They suddenly spring together.

Like poles (north-north or south-south) always repel each other.

South pole

South pole

2 Now try the same thing, with two south poles facing each other. The magnets twist away and force themselves apart.

Magnetic fields

An invisible "magnetic field" surrounds every magnet. You can use tiny pieces of iron, called iron filings, to find out where this field is. While the filings are in the magnetic field, they form a pattern around the magnet.

You will need:

Iron filings

Bar magnet

Plastic lid

1 Place the lid over the magnet.

2 Slowly sprinkle iron filings on the lid. Tap the lid gently from time to time.

3 The filings mark out the invisible magnetic field around the magnet.

The lines in the pattern show how the power of the magnet spreads out around it.

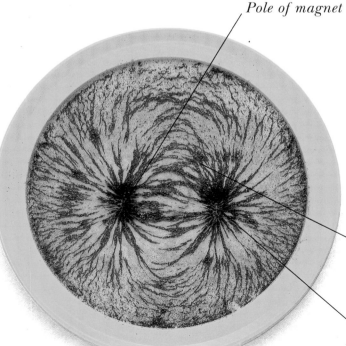

Pole of magnet

Pole of magnet

Fields in action

What happens to the magnetic fields when you bring two magnets together? Use iron filings to see how magnetic fields change as magnets attract or repel each other.

You will need:

Two bar magnets with their poles marked

Iron filings

1 Dip one magnet's north pole and another's south pole in the iron filings. Then bring the two poles together.

The magnetic fields around unlike poles join.

The iron filings are held in the magnetic field.

North pole

South pole

2 Pull the two magnets a short distance apart. The filings hang in the air!

North pole

North pole

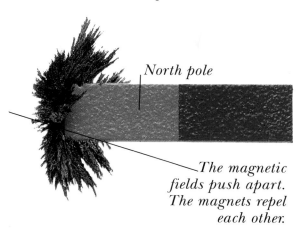

The magnetic fields push apart. The magnets repel each other.

3 Now try the same experiment again, but dip both north poles in the filings. This time, the filings bend away from each other.

Make a magnet

You can turn a needle and a paper clip into homemade magnets. But which is the north pole and which is the south pole of each magnet? Test them to find out, and then change the poles around.

You will need:

Tape

Compass

Bowl of water

Piece of cork cut into an arrow shape

Steel paper clip

Steel needle

Bar magnet with the poles marked

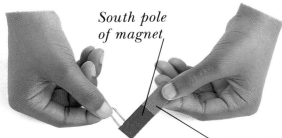

South pole of magnet

Take the magnet away from the paper clip between each stroke.

1 Stroke the paper clip about 20 times with the magnet's south pole. Stroke toward the point of the paper clip.

The arrow can also be made of styrofoam.

2 Tape the paper clip to the piece of cork. Float it in the water.

3 When the cork is still, use the compass to check that the point of the paper clip points north.

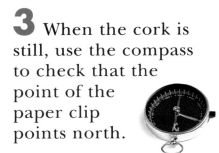

The paper clip has become a weak magnet with a north pole at its head.

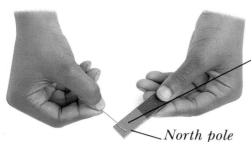

North pole

4 Stroke the eye of the needle with the north pole of the bar magnet. This makes it into a magnet.

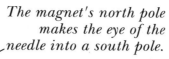

The magnet's north pole makes the eye of the needle into a south pole.

South pole

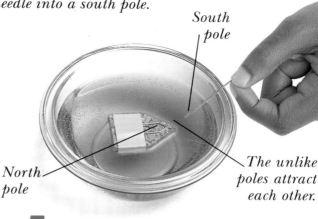

North pole

The unlike poles attract each other.

5 Bring the eye of the needle near the point of the paper clip. The paper clip turns toward the needle.

North pole

6 Now stroke the needle point with the magnet's north pole.

The like poles repel each other.

North pole

The point becomes a south pole, so the eye changes and becomes a north pole.

7 Bring the eye of the needle near the point of the paper clip again. The paper clip turns away.

Magnets in production
Magnets are made from steel. Molten steel is poured into molds and the steel is left to cool in a strong magnetic field. As the steel cools and hardens, it becomes magnetic.

Chain reaction

Magnetic fields can transform other things into magnets. See how ball bearings become magnetic while they are inside a magnetic field.

Bar magnet

Ball bearings

The magnetic field from the bar magnet makes each ball bearing magnetic.

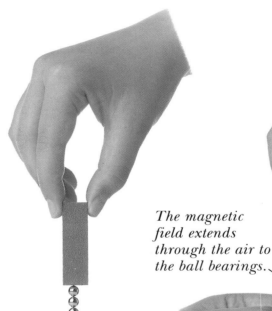

The magnetic field extends through the air to the ball bearings.

1 Place a ball bearing on the magnet. Add more bearings, one at a time.

2 The magnet holds the chain of ball bearings. Each bearing holds the one below it.

3 Hold the top ball bearing and slowly pull the magnet away. The ball bearings fall off, one by one.

Rob a magnet

It is sometimes hard to pull an object away from a powerful magnet because it grips the object with great force. Yet you can easily remove the object without even touching it. All you need is a nail.

You will need:

Ball bearing

Bar magnet

Nail

1 Make sure the nail is not already magnetic. It should not be able to pick up the ball bearing.

2 Pick up the ball bearing with the magnet.

3 Bring the point of the nail up to the ball bearing.

The magnetic field of the bar magnet passes into the nail and turns it into a stronger magnet. Because the nail is thinner, the magnetism is more concentrated.

4 Pull the nail away from the magnet. The ball bearing sticks to the nail.

Driving force

How can you drive a toy car without touching it? You can make a car and, using two bar magnets, learn about magnetism.

You will need:

Two bar magnets

Empty matchbox

Modeling clay

Drinking straw

Scissors

Two toothpicks

Tape

Piece of cardboard

Compass

1 Tape one of the magnets inside the matchbox tray.

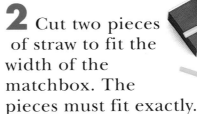

2 Cut two pieces of straw to fit the width of the matchbox. The pieces must fit exactly.

3 Tape the pieces of straw to the bottom of the matchbox. Slide in the tray.

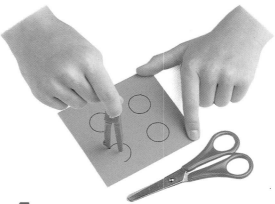

4 Using the compass, draw four small circles on the cardboard. Cut them out.

5 ⚠ Ask an adult to help you push the toothpicks through the straws and the centers of the cardboard circles. Put clay over the points of the toothpicks.

When you bring one north pole near the other, they repel each other and the car rolls away.

The same thing happens with the two south poles.

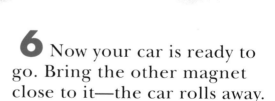

6 Now your car is ready to go. Bring the other magnet close to it—the car rolls away.

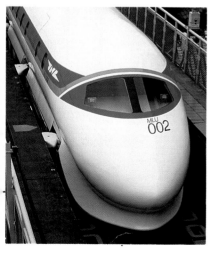

Floating train

This is a new kind of train that has no wheels. It runs without touching the track. Magnets in the train and in the track support the train and make it float above the track. The magnets also make the train move.

Electric magnet

You cannot turn off the magnetism in bar and horseshoe magnets. But you can make an electric magnet, or "electromagnet," that will switch on and off. This works because a magnetic field forms around a wire when electricity flows through it.

You will need:

6-volt battery

Large nail

Two used matchsticks

Thin wire

Pins

1 Check to see that the nail is not already magnetic. It should not be able to pick up the pins.

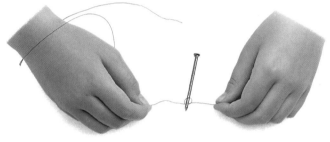

2 Tie the wire near the point of the nail.

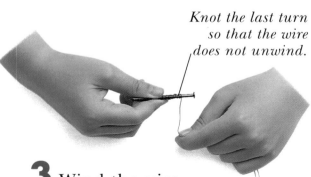

Knot the last turn so that the wire does not unwind.

3 Wind the wire tightly around the nail. Make about 100 turns, all in the same direction.

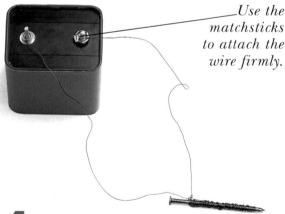

Use the matchsticks to attach the wire firmly.

4 Connect the end of each wire to a battery terminal.

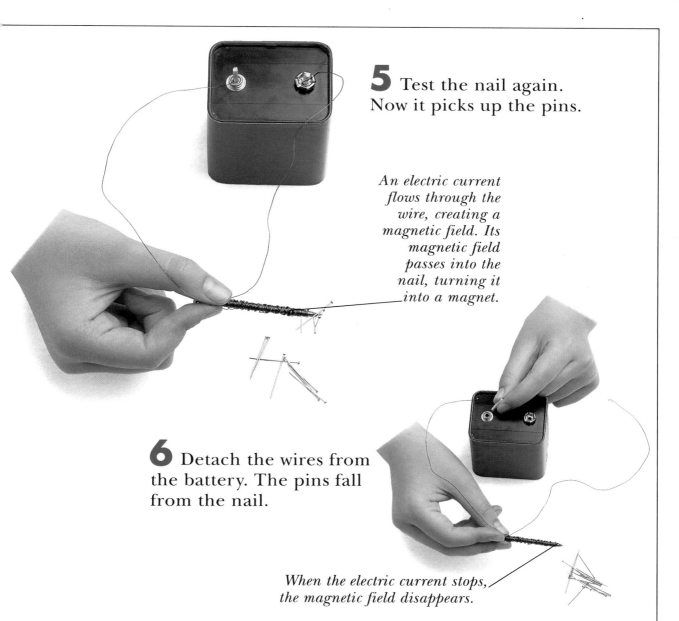

5 Test the nail again. Now it picks up the pins.

An electric current flows through the wire, creating a magnetic field. Its magnetic field passes into the nail, turning it into a magnet.

6 Detach the wires from the battery. The pins fall from the nail.

When the electric current stops, the magnetic field disappears.

Metal mover

Cranes use electromagnets to lift scrap iron and steel. A strong electric current flows through the electromagnet, the scrap sticks to the magnet, and the crane lifts it. When the current is switched off, the scrap metal falls.

Changing direction

Does an electromagnet have north and south poles like a bar magnet? You can use the floating magnet you made earlier to test your electromagnet and find out whether or not it has poles.

You will need:

Electromagnet and battery (pages 24–25)

Floating magnet (pages 18–19)

The point of the nail is the south pole. It attracts the floating magnet's north pole.

1 Hold the point of the electromagnet near the floating magnet.

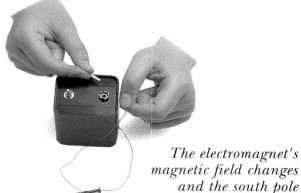

The electromagnet's magnetic field changes and the south pole becomes the north pole.

2 Now switch the wires around on the battery. The current flows in the opposite direction.

Now the floating magnet is repelled.

3 Test the electromagnet again.

Telephones
Telephones use electromagnets to create sound. Electricity passes through an electromagnet in the earpiece, causing it to vibrate and create the sounds we hear.

Magnets and motors

You can build a simple electric motor that shows how motors use magnetism. Real motors contain a coil of wire that spins smoothly. Yours will turn jerkily but will show you how an electric motor works.

You will need

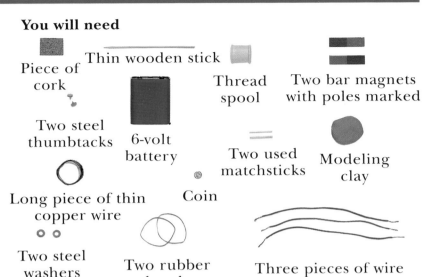

Piece of cork

Thin wooden stick

Thread spool

Two bar magnets with poles marked

Two steel thumbtacks

6-volt battery

Two used matchsticks

Modeling clay

Long piece of thin copper wire

Coin

Two steel washers

Two rubber bands

Three pieces of wire with bared ends

1 Hold the spool upright and wind the copper wire vertically around it. Leave the ends free.

2 Use rubber bands to hold the wire in place.

3 Push the stick through the spool.

Continued on next page

4 Wrap the ends of the copper wire around the washers and slip them onto the stick.

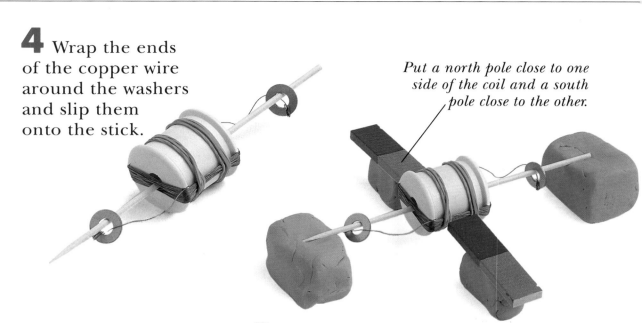

Put a north pole close to one side of the coil and a south pole close to the other.

5 Divide the clay into four pieces. Support the stick on two of these pieces. Use the other two to support two bar magnets, one on each side of the coil.

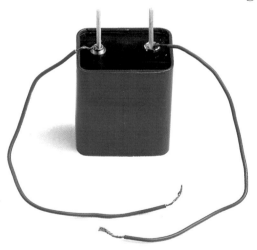

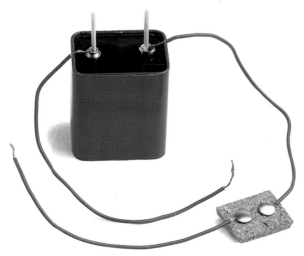

6 Use the matchsticks to attach two pieces of the coated wire to the battery.

7 Stick the thumbtacks in the cork. Attach the third piece of coated wire to one thumbtack. Attach one of the wires from the battery to the other.

28

Continued from previous page

8 Loop the two unconnected wire ends loosely around the washers. Touch the two thumbtacks with the coin. The spool will move.

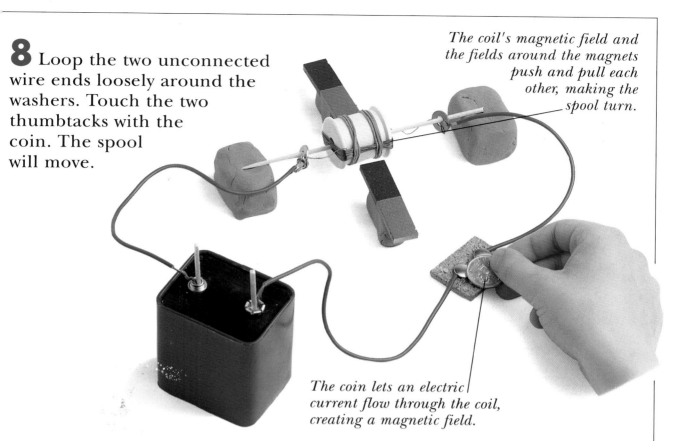

The coil's magnetic field and the fields around the magnets push and pull each other, making the spool turn.

The coin lets an electric current flow through the coil, creating a magnetic field.

Around the house

This electric drill uses an electric motor. The coil inside it spins when the current is switched on, turning the drill. Other electric machines in your home, such as vacuum cleaners and food processors, work in a similar way.

Picture credits
(Abbreviation key: B=below, C=center, L=left, R=right, T=top)

Ancient Art & Architecture Collection/ Ronald Sheridan: 6TR; Ardea London Limited/John Daniels: 7TL; Pete Gardner: 7CR, 9BL, 26BC; The Image Bank: 29CL; Dave King: 6BR; Rockwater: 13BL; Science Photo Library/Jack Finch: 6CL; Simon Fraser: 25BL; Swift Levick Magnets Limited: 19BL; Takeshi

Takahara: 23BL; Seaphot Limited/Planet Earth Pictures: 14BL

Picture research Paula Cassidy and Rupert Thomas

Production Louise Barratt

Dorling Kindersley would like to thank Claire Gillard for editorial assistance; H. Shaw (Magnets) Sheffield for supplying magnets; Mrs Bradbury, the

staff and children of Allfarthing Junior School, Wandsworth, especially Miriam Habtesellasse, Alistair Lambert, Lucy Martin, Sam Miller, Paul Nolan, Alan Penfold, Robin Raggett, and David Tross; Michael Brown, Mela Macgregor, Katie Martin, Susanna Scott, and Natasha Shepherd.